COUNSELLING YOUR STAFF

Better Management Skills

This highly popular range of inexpensive paperbacks covers all areas of basic management. Practical, easy to read and instantly accessible, these guides will help managers to improve their business or communication skills. Those marked * are available on audio cassette.

The books in this series can be tailored to specific company requirements. For further details, please contact the publisher, Kogan Page, telephone 0171-278 0433, fax 0171-837 6348.

Be a Successful Supervisor
Business Etiquette
Coaching Your Employees
Creative Decision-making
Creative Thinking in Business
Delegating for Results
Effective Employee Participation
Effective Meeting Skills
Effective Performance Appraisals*
Effective Presentation Skills
Empowerment
First Time Supervisor
Get Organised!
Goals and Goal Setting
How to Communicate Effectively*
How to Develop a Positive Attitude*
How to Develop Assertiveness
How to Motivate People*
How to Understand Financial Statements
How to Write a Staff Manual
Improving Employee Performance
Improving Relations at Work
Keeping Customers for Life
Leadership Skills for Women
Learning to Lead
Make Every Minute Count*
Managing Disagreement Constructively
Managing Organisational Change
Managing Part-Time Employees
Managing Quality Customer Service
Managing Your Boss
Marketing for Success
Memory Skills in Business
Mentoring
Office Management
Productive Planning
Project Management
Quality Customer Service
Rate Your Skills as a Manager
Sales Training Basics
Self-managing Teams
Selling Professionally
Speed Reading in Business
Successful Negotiation
Successful Telephone Techniques
Systematic Problem-solving and Decision-making
Team Building
Training Methods that Work

COUNSELLING YOUR STAFF

Warren Redman

First published in 1995

Apart from any fair dealing for the purposes of research or private study, or criticism or review, as permitted under the Copyright, Designs and Patents Act, 1988, this publication may only be reproduced, stored or transmitted, in any form or by any means, with the prior permission in writing of the publishers, or in the case of reprographic reproduction in accordance with the terms of licences issued by the Copyright Licensing Agency. Enquiries concerning reproduction outside those terms should be sent to the publishers at the undermentioned address:

Kogan Page Limited
120 Pentonville Road
London N1 9JN

© Warren Redman 1995

The right of Warren Redman to be identified as author of this work has been asserted by him in accordance with the Copyright, Designs and Patents Act 1988.

British Library Cataloguing in Publication Data

A CIP record for this book is available from the British Library.

ISBN 0-7494-1564-9

Typeset by BookEns Ltd, Royston, Herts.
Printed and bound in Great Britain by Clays Ltd, St Ives plc

Contents

Introduction   11

1. Who This Book is For   13
Managers of others *13*
People who have been asked to take on a counselling role *14*
What this book can do *14*
What this book can't do *16*
Your role as a counsellor *17*
NVQ competences *18*

2. Why Counselling is an Important Management Task   19
Stress *19*
Illness *20*
Absenteeism *21*
Low motivation *21*
Poor work *22*
High staff turnover *23*
What it costs *23*
A cost-effective, preventive measure *24*
A response to a crisis *25*
Making a case for counselling *25*

3. What Counselling Is – and Isn't   27
A definition of counselling *27*

A longer-term development process *28*
What counselling is *29*
What counselling isn't *30*
Counselling situations *30*
Comments *32*

4. **The Skills of Counselling**   34
Some background *34*
Relationship skills *34*
Listening skills *35*
Asking appropriate questions *35*
Diagnostic skills *36*
Confidentiality *36*
Contract-setting *37*
Refraining skills *37*
Intervention skills *38*
Self-awareness *38*
Empathy *39*
Objectivity *39*
Referral skills *40*
Summary *40*

5. **A Structure for Listening**   42
Listening is a process *42*
To listen: set a contract *43*
To hear: identify the issue *43*
To understand: clarify what is presented *44*
To accept: summarise what is being said *45*
To respond: agree appropriate action *46*
The structure *46*
Task *47*

6. **Asking Questions**   48
Types of question *48*
Open questions *48*
Closed questions *49*
Mirror or reflecting questions *49*
Probing questions *50*

Leading questions 51
Qualified questions 51
Multiple questions 51
Task 51

7. **Signals and Messages**   53
   Non-verbal signals and body language 53
   Exercise 53
   Making a message from the signals 54
   Responding to the message 56
   Task 57

8. **A Structure for a Counselling Interview**   58
   Setting the scene 58
   Establishing the contract 59
   The presenting issue 59
   Observing and reflecting back 60
   Clarifying the key points 60
   Summarising and closing 61
   The length and frequency of sessions 61
   Erica's problem 62
   Task 67

9. **Taking and Keeping Notes**   68
   Why take notes? 68
   When to take notes 69
   What kind of notes to take 70
   Who are the notes for? 70
   How and where to keep records 71
   Task 72

10. **Who Should be the Counsellor?**   73
    The manager? 73
    Someone not in a direct managerial position? 74
    Someone designated as a counsellor? 75
    Task 76

11. Training for the Counsellor   77
Resources *77*
Practice and experience *78*
Getting feedback *80*
Task *81*

12. Supervision and Support   82
Counselling can be lonely *82*
Carrying other people's burdens *83*
Finding support *83*
What counselling supervision is; where to find it *84*
Task *85*

13. Counselling Issues and Situations   86
A drink problem *87*
Relationships (personal and work) *88*
Employment problems *88*
Marital problems *89*
Bereavement and loss *90*
Trauma *90*
Family difficulties (children, parents, partners) *91*
Alcohol and drug misuse *91*
Health concerns (such as cancer, AIDS etc) *91*
Task *92*

14. A Code of Practice for Counselling   94
Activity *94*
Exercise *96*
A code of practice *97*
Confidentiality *97*
Relationships *97*
Giving advice *98*
Initiating the counselling process *98*
Task *99*

15. Setting Up a Counselling Programme   100
Considerations *100*
A plan *101*

Keeping records *101*
Evaluating the programme *102*

16. Open for Business! 103
What to say *103*
Where to offer counselling *104*
Being patient *104*

17. Evaluating the Counselling Programme 106
Defining your aim *106*
How to measure success *107*

18. A Checklist 109
Key points to remember *109*
Task *110*
Finally *110*

Appendix *112*
Further reading *112*
Some national referral agencies *112*

Introduction

We have all been counselled at some time. We have all counselled somebody else. It probably hasn't been called that, it was just something that happened as part of two people talking. You might recall some of those conversations.

The question is, was that counselling a helpful, positive experience (for both parties), or do you see it now as unhelpful and negative? Of course, it may have been totally forgettable.

Here's a clue. If the person getting counselled felt *listened to, heard and understood, accepted and responded to*, and went away feeling a little more confident and able to get on with the day, then something positive happened. If the person going away thought, 'I could never do that, that counsellor may be clever, but she (or he) just didn't understand', then something's gone wrong.

If you're reading this book, you are probably a manager and you have probably realised that you do some counselling. Now you want to find out something about it. Congratulations! Counselling is a powerful and beneficial tool for any manager, both for the individual being counselled and for the organisation itself. That is, if it's done well.

You may know enough about counselling to regard it as something that only professionals do, that requires years of training and has a great deal of mystique and 'psychology' attached to it. You'd be partly right, but don't let it put you off any more.

Counselling Your Staff

Counselling is part of any positive, healthy, human interaction. People talk about themselves, their concerns, what's holding them back. Others listen and respond in a way that enables some resolution to be found.

Or do they? One of the things holding back individuals and organisations is that nobody seems to listen to anyone else. Nobody grows, learning to use their full potential. Problems remain unresolved, leaving poor work relationships, dissatisfied personnel, anger and bitterness, usually unspoken.

This book will help you to see counselling as a straightforward process and that while it demands skill and understanding it can and should be undertaken by every manager in the workplace.

CHAPTER 1
Who This Book is For

Managers of others

You don't have to be called a manager to manage others. When it comes to counselling, the important thing is that you feel you have some responsibility for the well-being and healthy productiveness of those around you; and that you have some authority to do something about it.

If you are a manager, in real terms if not in name, this book will introduce you not only to counselling but also to some of the basic skills you need to manage any member of staff.

There's one proviso though: if you're the sort of manager who believes that staff just need telling what to do and that they are basically an ill-disciplined lazy lot if left to their own devices, the counselling approach isn't for you. Since you've picked up this book, there's a good chance that you are of the opinion that people are, generally speaking, self-motivating and willing to get on with things when they have the opportunity, and you understand that sometimes they need a little help to deal with difficulties that may confront them.

So, to be more specific, this book is for the manager who already has an optimistic as well as a realistic viewpoint about his or her staff.

People who have been asked to take on a counselling role

Even if you're not a manager, you may have been asked to carry out some counselling. This is an increasing trend in organisations of all types and sizes.

> One organisation employing several thousand people recognised that absenteeism and accidents accounted for a considerable portion of avoidable waste. It set up a counselling programme and invited interested staff to become counsellors. These people were given some training and asked to counsel other members of staff. Counsellors were drawn from management and supervisory staff as well as administrative and manual workers.

There could be a much more informal process than the above illustration, especially in smaller organisations. In one company of about 30 people, Eileen the office manager was asked to 'see' people from time to time when there seemed to be a problem. It wasn't just the function that she had, it was more to do with her style, which made people want to talk to Eileen. Instead of seeing this as a potential problem, the senior manager used Eileen's natural talent to ensure that people with problems had a listening ear.

Maybe you, like Eileen, have been asked to 'do some counselling' (even if the word counselling wasn't used). But then what? This book will help you to know where to start and how to carry out effective and beneficial counselling.

What this book can do

You already have a whole range of qualities and skills that you apply to your work with others; probably many more than you realise. Whatever you have, counselling will add to those skills and give you competences that can be used far more widely than within a formal counselling session with a member

Who This Book is For

of staff. For instance, your interviewing skills, your negotiating skills and your general ability to interact on a personal level with other people will be greatly enhanced. You will be in demand!

It might be helpful for you at this stage to consider some of your skills and what you want to concentrate on. You may be good at some things and want to develop and improve on those particular strengths. You might have some skills that you feel are weak. Note them down here and make your use of this book more relevant to your own needs so that, rather than me telling you what you should be doing (bad counselling practice), you will be defining for yourself your own needs and interests and creating your own learning contract. (You will already have gathered from this that the person *being counselled* has to do most of the work, not the counsellor.)

My skills with people	What I want to improve

The skills of counselling that you can gain from reading this book and trying out the exercises and processes will add to what you already have. You will find that those skills, and the understanding that comes with them, help you to widen your own repertoire considerably.

Not only will you become more adept and confident at counselling; you will find that this helps you in your daily contact with other people in many circumstances.

It's no coincidence that the people I know who are good counsellors are self-confident, can relate to other people easily, are held in high regard by others and usually are successful in a range of activities. Starting out on the trail towards becoming competent at counselling can therefore lead to your achieving personal success in other areas of your work and life.

What this book can't do

Working with this book will give you some basic tools and guidelines for counselling staff. Simply reading it won't. You will need to practise by carrying out the exercises. Keep the book by you as a reference point, always remembering that there is no substitute for experience.

In any event, this book does not pretend to turn you into a 'professional' counsellor. It will help you to gain the required competence, should you need it, to carry out counselling under the National Vocational Qualification scheme through the Management Charter Initiative (see NVQ criteria on page 18). But it won't give you an accreditation as a recognised counsellor through, for example, the British Association for Counselling. For that, you need to undertake a rigorous programme of training and self-development, including many hours of supervised counselling.

Many organisations do offer training. If you wanted to go further than this book will take you, there are plenty of opportunities to do so.

This book won't make any assumptions about your prior experience or training as a counsellor. You may be starting out fresh or you might have plenty of experience and want to

Who This Book is For

hone the skills you already have.

If this is the first book on counselling that you've read, use it as a starting point. Later on, if you wish, you can expand on the issues presented here through the many books available, mainly aimed at the person whose key role is as a counsellor. If you already have other more weighty volumes, use this as a handy reference point to check out the practice of counselling your staff. See the appendix for a brief reading list and addresses of some national organisations.

Your role as a counsellor

To summarise, think about what your own role is in offering counselling to staff. Have you decided to carry out some counselling as part of your duties as a responsible manager? Perhaps you've been asked to counsel other members of staff. Do you find that people converge on you because you're good at listening to them and you think you could develop this as a skill? Have you recognised some specific problems among your staff and want to carry out counselling as a way of resolving them?

Have a go at defining your role, in a way that will help you to describe it to someone else. First an example is given; then write in your own definition of your role.

Peter's role

I'm manager of a team of engineers. I have many roles with them; as leader, recruiter, quality controller, coach, motivator, project supervisor, for example. I also act as a counsellor. That's when I'll make some time just to listen to some of the problems and concerns that people on the team bring me. They know that I won't judge them. We'll deal with things on a personal level and entirely in confidence.

Counselling Your Staff

My role

_____

_____

_____

NVQ competences

If you want to gain a credit through the NVQ scheme you will need to demonstrate the required competences. Here are the desired performance criteria to counsel staff, taken from the Occupational Standards for Managers. (Management I.)

- Counselling takes place in a private place at a time appropriate to the type, seriousness and complexity of the problem.
- Counselling practices and processes conform to any relevant personnel policies of the organisation.
- All discussions with individuals are designed to encourage and assist them to take responsibility for their own decisions and actions.
- In cases where the manager's personal skills and knowledge are insufficient, an appropriate counselling service is recommended to the individual.
- Individual cases are sufficiently monitored to make sure that a positive outcome is reached.

CHAPTER 2
Why Counselling is an Important Management Task

Not so long ago counselling was seen as a 'soft' and marginal practice, only to be found in the welfare departments of larger organisations and it is still seen that way in many unenlightened places of work. More companies began to accept counselling as a method of dealing with their own guilt when it came to large-scale redundancies, in an attempt (usually too late) to assist staff in finding new careers.

Counselling can not only deal with many staff problems; it also brings significant beneficial economic results to the organisation. According to the UK Health and Safety Executive, the cost of occupational stress in terms of sickness absence alone is about £4 billion per annum, not counting other forms of lost productive value.

Just consider some of the symptoms of frustration being shown by people known to you, possibly working within your own organisation. Then do some quick sums to see the effect of those symptoms on the well-being of the organisation itself.

Stress

People experience stress when they have more frustration than they can handle. Often the stress is self-imposed, although it is usually attributed to external factors. Those factors may be personal; for example bereavement, divorce or other major life changes; or they may be to do with work: the fear of redundancy, changes in the structure or working practices, anxiety about being able to achieve what is expected, bad relationships within the workplace.

Some people thrive on pressure. That's when they seem to achieve the most. Others may find the same pressure too much, so that they become paralysed or ineffective. This is when pressure turns into stress. What the manager has to be aware of is when this change occurs. The person who has always operated well under pressure may suddenly find everything too much. The busy person piles on the work until nothing can be done properly, then explodes. Another common occurrence is that this same person finds it hard to cope well when things are apparently quiet. Instead of using that time to plan ahead, he or she becomes disruptive or morose.

The person who has an apparent low threshold of pressure may have a different pattern of working that might still be very productive as long as this is recognised.

In all circumstances of stress, while there are usually external factors that you may be unable to change, counselling can help individuals to deal with how they feel and to be able to reach a constructive and positive form of action. In other words, reducing the stress people feel amounts to more efficient and productive use of human resources.

While stress is a symptom of a person's frustration, through some change that is difficult to cope with, there are a number of symptoms that indicate when a person is under stress.

Illness

A clear link has been shown between stress and illness. Backaches, stomach-aches and other internal physical problems, headaches and migraine, tiredness and depressive or other mental illnesses might all be related to each other and to the incidence of stress in a person's life.

Our bodies and our minds are constantly sending each other

messages. At the simplest level, just think about a time when you experienced some stress. Perhaps you stood up to talk to a large group of people for the first time, went for an interview, had an argument, got married, gave up smoking. How did you feel? Did you have any physical symptoms? Sweaty palms, headaches, nausea, neckache, for example? If so, multiply this by a few times and you might see how easy it is for people to become quite ill from being under stress. If you didn't experience any of this, you are probably unique in the history of humankind.

Absenteeism

The number of days lost through illness, much of which can be attributed to stress, is significant enough to cause an increasing number of businesses and other organisations to establish counselling programmes. The primary reason is not an overwhelming desire to be nice to people. It is to reduce the number of working days lost and increase the efficiency and productivity of personnel.

People often absent themselves from work, giving illness as an excuse, when the real reason is a temporary inability to cope with work or personal pressures, perhaps from a bad relationship with the manager. Signs of such dissatisfaction indicate, not that the staff needs counselling, but that the manager might.

Low motivation

Change of any kind can induce stress, especially when this change is outside the control of the individual. In turn, this may lead to a lack of willingness to carry out work as effectively as possible.

Low motivation is a common symptom of a person experiencing some problems. It is seldom, if ever, a natural part of a person's make-up. People are motivated when they are heard and feel themselves to be a valuable and respected part of a group. They usually are motivated when they feel they have some control over decisions and actions for which they are responsible.

The effect of low motivation among staff is that managers are faced with extra work, disciplinary action, constant frustration. It tends to become a vicious circle, with everyone eventually reducing their motivation to perform well.

Poor work

The results of stress, illness, absenteeism and lack of motivation are inevitable. They add up to poor work. Customers will experience the effects. Profits will fall.

Errors and inadequacies may be due to a variety of reasons. Training might be insufficient, work might be organised inappropriately, communication may be poor. Those things need to be attended to, since they indicate management ineffectiveness, rather than individual staff being sloppy. Once again, it's the managers who might need counselling.

However, where you notice that a person whom you regard as capable is turning out uncharacteristically bad work, this may be a signal that something is going wrong in that individual's work or personal life. Getting to the root of poor work being produced and being aware of changes in people's behaviour is vital if you are to focus your attention on counselling as a tool for improving performance.

> A thousand pairs of shoes were returned to one factory after the customer complained of a fault. The operator who had carried out the offending application was reprimanded, but claimed that she was working under pressure with a defective design. The designer had made a miscalculation. He had been unable to concentrate properly, he said, because his baby son had just been taken to hospital and he was having to look after his two other children while his wife stayed at the hospital. He wished he had been able to talk to someone about it. It cost the factory about £25,000 and the loss of a major customer.

High staff turnover

People leave their employment for all sorts of reasons. If your organisation has a higher than average staff turnover, you may need to look at the reasons behind it. Some movement of staff is a healthy part of the organisation's as well as the individual's development. But people often leave because they are dissatisfied or unhappy with their work, the people around them, the unrealistic expectations of them and, most commonly among the most able people, the lack of responsibility and opportunities for initiative they are given.

The costs of any staff changes are far higher than the costs of attending to staff who would otherwise stay and continue to give added value. Listening to staff, helping them to overcome problems that they may be facing while at the same time taking account of general changes that are needed, are all potentially beneficial results of counselling.

What it costs

Rather than give a very general and therefore not very helpful or relevant cost/benefit analysis of counselling, here is an exercise you can do to enable you and your colleagues to become clearer about the costs to your own organisation.

First, decide how you can best get the statistics. You are probably better off looking at a typical segment of the organisation, then multiplying by the proportionate number of people working for the organisation as a whole. You might also want to look at a month, or a three-month period rather than a year, then multiply by twelve or four to get the annual figures.

Look at the numbers and the costs to the organisation of absenteeism, poor work, staff turnover over the past year. You will have to decide how to make the calculations. If your business makes or sells goods, for example, poor work can be measured by returns, duplicated work, repair time, cancelled orders and so on. If you are a service organisation, you may have to look at complaints, waiting time, loss of customers and so on. Calculate all the staff time (and therefore costs) as well as material wastage and loss of profits on an order. Don't forget the costs of engaging and training new staff to replace those who have left.

Symptom	Time cost	Material cost	Overall cost
Absenteeism			
Poor work			
Staff turnover			
Other			

Not all of this could have been eliminated by counselling. From your own knowledge and experience, however, give some thought to some of the circumstances that you can identify. Then make some calculation as to the proportion of savings that might have been made by listening to people properly before errors, absenteeism or resignations took place.

A cost-effective, preventive measure

The argument for counselling your staff is that it is a cost-effective way of preventing disasters before they take place. That is as true for the organisation as it is for the individual being counselled.

Counselling, especially in the workplace, is not only a way of helping people to solve their problems, it is a way of strengthening relationships between people, clarifying where staff need particular support, identifying needs for changes in the workplace and creating an atmosphere of trust and care within the organisation. In other words, it is a way of acknowledging and valuing the people who work with you.

This is what improves motivation of staff and enhances their performance.

A response to a crisis

Individuals usually seek counselling when they are at a crisis point. This means that counselling has to be available when the person needs it. The problem with this is that organisations usually offer counselling when they have initiated a crisis themselves.

While there are many professionals and agencies offering counselling, those who need it seldom have easy access to them or even know anything about them. People in work who are in crisis could find it far easier and appropriate to go to a designated person within the workplace. Organisations that offer counselling as part of the process of management will be able to respond to people going through a difficult time, when they need help.

The more common organisational response, however, is one that 'brings in' counselling when there has been a big redundancy or redeployment programme, or a restructuring that causes significant turbulence to employees. This is not the mark of a healthy or positive approach. For counselling to work properly to the benefit of both employee and organisation, it should be readily available as a normal part of what managers do.

This means that counselling is most effective when it is part of the culture of the organisation. As with all cultural changes, this takes time. Setting up any counselling process, therefore, takes considerable patience, acceptance at all levels within the organisation, and attention to detail.

The first step is to establish your case for counselling, or if there is already an accepted counselling process, to understand what the case is.

Making a case for counselling

Imagine you are to present a case to the boss. Your mandate is to show why and how counselling might be an important part of the management process, in economic terms. The cost of counselling will be the time taken by managers and staff to

Counselling Your Staff

include any training that is needed by managers. Consider your own circumstances, the issues facing the organisation and the loss in profits due to such things as absenteeism, staff turnover and poor work.

Write down the headings here, to help you to make your case for counselling.

_____

_____

_____

_____

_____

CHAPTER 3
What Counselling Is – and Isn't

A definition of counselling

First try saying what you believe counselling to be. Just jot down your own definition here; it will probably be helpful when you come to compare it with the issues raised in this chapter.

_____

_____

_____

There are a number of ways to define counselling. Even professional counselling organisations, like the British Association for Counselling, find it difficult to come up with one precise definition, so if you find it hard, you're not alone. All counselling agencies and professionals agree on one thing, however: except in specific circumstances, counselling is *not* advice giving, despite the common misconception that this is precisely what it is.

So, if you have given a definition that talks about counselling primarily as giving advice, please think again. Try writing down another definition that omits any mention of advice.

A longer-term development process

Here is my definition of counselling:

> Counselling is a process of clarifying a problem held by another person(s), enabling them to take appropriate responsibility for that problem, and then assisting them to arrive at some form of resolution of the difficulty.
>
> As such, counselling is seen as a longer-term development process.

There are a number of important implications if you accept this definition of counselling:

- Counselling is a *process*, not a technique or a once-off, quick-fix answer to people's problems.
- Counselling is about helping somebody else to *clarify*, that is to make sense of what his or her problem is.
- Counselling is about getting the person with the problem to accept *responsibility* for it where that is appropriate. If it's not their responsibility, then it's not their problem and the counselling is aimed at helping them to recognise and accept that. What this means, is that we need to help people get to the root of what their problem is. So, for example, if the person's 'problem' is stated as 'I can't stand the way my boss treats me', there are two separate issues. One is that it seems as though the boss has the problem (although he or she may not see that). Second, the staff member may need to deal with the issue of personal self-esteem, or guilt at not being able to deal with the boss.

- Counselling should always lead to a *resolution* of the problem. In this last one, always remember that a resolution is seldom to be found in the giving of any answers or advice. There is a place for advice giving; but that isn't counselling. Where the real problem is something like dealing with unwarranted guilt or low self-esteem, no amount of advice will change that.

What counselling is

Study the above definition of counselling carefully. How does it relate to your own understanding of what counselling is? If you have significant differences of opinion, give some thought to what you have actually described. If you accept my definition as close to your own perception, what follows will help you to carry it forward.

While counselling may be seen as giving guidance, it is guidance given in a way that leads the staff member to his or her own understanding of the problem and towards taking the action that will solve it. That is why counselling is a longer-term development process. If you simply told people how to solve their personal problems (in the nicest possible way), they may take your advice, but it's doubtful whether they would have learned to take responsibility for dealing with their own problems in the future.

The applications of the counselling process range from helping your staff to resolve problems of relationships or addictive behaviour to simply listening and allowing them to vent everyday frustrations.

In order to carry out the process of counselling effectively, you will have developed your mental, imaginative and emotional powers to quite a high degree. In other words, you need to be able to observe and analyse, visualise and be creative, have empathy and understand your own feelings.

What counselling isn't

You will already have seen that counselling is neither giving advice nor solving other people's problems for them. If you are that kind of manager, you will not be in the business of assisting your staff to develop their own potential. More likely, your staff will be disgruntled because they never learn anything and you will be rushed off your feet doing other people's work for them.

In that respect, the counselling approach is similar to the skills of coaching, where you will be assisting staff to discover their own solutions. The difference is that counselling is usually a response to a staff member's personal problem.

You can deal with those personal problems in a number of ways. One way is to set up a disciplinary process. Counselling is often seen as something that 'somebody needs' in order to prevent them from carrying out unacceptable behaviour. Counselling is not a disciplinary interview. The outcome of such an interview may lead to the staff member realising that there is a problem and asking for some help. But please do not confuse the two by pretending to offer counselling when you really want to discipline somebody.

A general rule that will tell you whether you are in a position to be offering to counsel a staff member is to ask who is setting the agenda. If you want to be giving your (or the company's) point of view; if you want to offer your advice or information about an aspect of the person's behaviour; if you have a complaint to make, then this is your agenda and it's inappropriate for you to offer counselling. If you are open to the staff member bringing you his or her concerns and problems, are able to give sufficient time and attention to these concerns and are just prepared to listen without judgement, then it looks as though you are about to offer some counselling support.

Counselling situations

Here are two examples of potential counselling scenarios. Jot

What Counselling Is – and Isn't

down your response to them. Are they both appropriate for counselling? How would you handle them?

> Marcus approaches you in your office. He asks if you could spare a minute, then says he'd like a couple of days' leave because he has to move home. When you ask him more about it, he reveals that he and his wife are going through a divorce and he is moving out, leaving his two young children with his wife and going to a small flat on the other side of town. 'I just need a couple of days', he says, 'I'll be quite all right after I've settled in. Don't worry, it won't affect my work and I'll make up the time.'

Your response:

_____
_____
_____

> Sarah stops you in the corridor. 'Look', she says, 'I wish you'd do something about Marcia. She keeps disappearing and wandering off. I found her in the washroom for the third time today. All she says is that she needs the time to think and that she can't do her work without thinking. But she won't talk about it and I think she's got a problem. Anyway, she's not pulling her weight and it's not fair to the others.'

Your response:

_____
_____
_____

Comments

In the first example, Marcus may well need the support that counselling can give him. As the manager, you could simply respond to his request for two days' leave. This may be all that Marcus requires from you to arrange his affairs. As someone prepared and able to offer counselling, you might also be the most appropriate person to help him go through a difficult personal time and one that might well disrupt his work, whatever he says at this point.

He has chosen to confide in you already. This is sufficient reason to believe that he would find it helpful to talk it through with you at greater length if you show that you are prepared to listen.

In the second example, you might take this further as a disciplinary matter and see it as nothing more. A warning to Marcia, once you have established that Sarah has been accurate in what she has said, could be sufficient to change her behaviour. But there may be much more to this. If you take a counselling approach, you are more likely to ask Marcia what is bothering her and whether she would like to talk about it in confidence. If she understands what you are offering, she knows that she has the option to take up counselling. It is up to her how she responds.

Now make a note of some counselling situations from your own experience. Don't use real names, and disguise the actual events if necessary. They may be situations where you had, or could have done with, some counselling in the past, or where you offered, or might have offered counselling to someone else.

1. _____

_____

_____

_____

What Counselling Is – and Isn't

2. _____
   _____
   _____
   _____

3. _____
   _____
   _____
   _____

CHAPTER 4
The Skills of Counselling

Some background

Counselling probably springs from two sources. The first is the normal human responses that helping people have always given to others. The second springs from the original work of Sigmund Freud and Carl Jung and their followers.

There are many schools of counselling and a plethora of approaches. They include the Gestalt approach of Fritz Perls, Transactional Analysis, developed by Eric Berne, the psychodynamic approach favoured by many therapists and the person-centred approach of Carl Rogers. If you are starting out, you won't need to learn all these approaches, although it's helpful to know that they exist. What is important and common to all approaches are the basic skills needed to carry out any counselling.

Relationship skills

You don't need to be the life and soul of the party, in fact this wouldn't be a helpful attribute for a counsellor; but you do need to be someone who can communicate with people at an individual level.

This means that you need to be genuinely interested in other people. The person who is purely ego centred, or self-interested, is not likely to come across as open and trustworthy. In order to make satisfactory relationships of any kind, you must be able to give acknowledgement to the other person and to show that you value them. This means putting your own interests on the back burner for at least half of the time. In counselling, your own interests should be entirely secondary to those of the person being counselled.

Listening skills

This is the key skill in counselling. In fact, it is probably the key skill in almost any management or person-centred activity. If you can get this one right, you have an immensely powerful and positive tool with which to succeed and to help others succeed.

However good you think you are at listening, you will certainly need to gain additional practice in order to counsel anybody. The next chapter deals with this skill in a little more depth. For now, I suggest that you try this out. Think of a conversation that you had in the last couple of hours or so. Jot down the main things that the other person conveyed to you.

Asking appropriate questions

In order to listen to what the person is really saying and to help that person towards some resolution, you will need to ask questions. The timing and the type of those questions, as well as the way you ask them, will determine how helpful you are.

Too many or too few questions, put in an inappropriate way or at the wrong time, will have the effect of putting off the other person and counteract your good listening. Chapter 6 deals with the various types of question. Before then, just write down here a few notes on the kinds of question you're aware of and what you believe is appropriate in the counselling setting. You might want to link it with real examples from the conversation you have just recorded.

Type of question	Example/s

Diagnostic skills

You are not expected to make a diagnosis on the state of mental or physical health of the person you are counselling. That is definitely the province of a professionally qualified person. What you do need is an ability to analyse what is being presented to you, to make sense of it and to be able to respond accordingly.

Chapter 7, Signals and Messages, has more to say on this aspect.

Confidentiality

The essence of a counselling session is that it is confidential. That has to be made quite clear at the beginning of any session with the staff member being counselled. It's an issue that has caused much debate, so you will have to be certain about any departures from this rule and make them explicit to anyone whom you counsel.

Consider whether there are any instances where, in your case within the organisation, you would not be bound to maintain confidentiality. If there are any circumstances, include them in this exercise. Write down a summary of what you would say to a member of staff coming to you for counselling in relation to the confidential nature of that counselling.

Contract-setting

You need to include more than just statements about confidentiality in any initial discussion about counselling. It is very likely that anyone coming for counselling for the first time will have no idea what to expect or what the rules are.

Where you are counselling staff it is even more important than usual to make it very clear what the person should expect, how you will be working, what your role is and many of the little, but crucial details. For example, how long a session might be, how many sessions and how regularly they occur, where you will meet, what you'll do about interruptions and so on. There may be things that the member of staff wants to say as well, so you should give him or her a chance to ask questions or add any further rules. This is the contract between you. Write down here what you will include in a contract and how you will include the wishes of the staff member.

Refraining skills

Part of asking the right questions at the right time is knowing when to refrain from asking or saying anything. Remember that the most important part of counselling is to listen to the other person. For that you must suspend your own judgement or thoughts about what you might do or what your experience is.

Since counselling is not giving advice, you might sometimes wonder what you are supposed to say when someone shares a problem with you. Whenever you are tempted to give an answer, or to talk about a similar experience that you had, or if you find your head whirling with ideas, the best thing to do is nothing.

Knowing when to hold back and being able to do so is an underused and considerable skill. Your response always needs to have the aim of helping the other person to make progress. Keeping quiet, while being attentive, can often be the catalyst to that progress. Regard the time you have with the staff member as that person's time to talk about the things that he or she really needs to share.

Intervention skills

There are times when you will need to stop the person from talking. This is when you recognise that the staff member is just going round in circles, repeating lengthy descriptions of similar circumstances or bemoaning his or her fate as though there is nothing that they could ever do about it.

At such points, you need to be strongly, but gently assertive; bringing the person back to hear what they have been saying and repeating, several times if needed, that they continue to return to the same issues without making the connection between them or taking responsibility for changing things.

Self-awareness

It's unlikely that you can be of any help to anyone else in counselling if you are not aware of your own strengths and weaknesses, your values and emotions, your likes and prejudices. An important part of the training for counsellors is that they have counselling themselves as part of their own development programme. So you don't need problems to have counselling.

Make a note about some of the things you know about yourself. You might find it helpful to go back to the skills list you did in Chapter 1 (page 15) as a starting point. This time concentrate on your personality, your positive and negative attributes, the kind of people you like and dislike.

_____

_____

_____

_____

_____

Empathy

This is a word much used in counselling, but not generally understood. It means having the ability to understand and accept the feelings of another person. It is not the same as feeling sympathetic, although it's close to that. Once you feel sorry for someone, it becomes hard to counsel them. But it is also hard to counsel someone if you have no grasp of how they are feeling.

Carl Rogers, who founded the 'person-centred' school of counselling, believed that empathy was the essential attribute needed in order to offer positive counselling support to another person.

Objectivity

You are treading a tightrope, trying to balance a whole range of skills here. While you need empathy, you also need to be objective. Once you start to get involved in other people's problems you have lost the ability to counsel them. All that you end up with are two people sharing the same problem. You might even finish up feeling worse than the person you're trying to help.

So, be with the person, but remain separate from his or her

problem. Remember that it's that person's issue, not yours. Also remember that the moment you start to make judgements, or to show in any way that you disapprove of the person's actions or behaviour, you are no longer able to counsel him or her.

Referral skills

There is much debate as to whether or not you need to know about a subject before being able to counsel somebody. For example, do you need to know about teenagers in order to counsel someone who is having a problem with a teenage child? Do you need to be an expert on AIDS to counsel someone concerned about that? Do you have to know about alcoholism to assist someone with an addictive drink problem?

My answer is no, you don't need to be an expert in all or any of those things in order to counsel somebody. But you do need to be aware of your limitations and have access to people or agencies who can provide such specialist guidance when that is needed. Always be clear about your own role and the contract you have with the person being counselled. When someone needs and is prepared to take other support, give the information about the relevant agency, while maintaining your own support for as long as is appropriate.

Your best source of information is a combination of the *Yellow Pages* and your local library.

Summary

Make a note here of the skills needed for counselling, relating them to your own abilities and what you now recognise you need to develop in yourself.

The Skills of Counselling

Skills	What/How I need to develop
Relationship skills	
Listening skills	
Asking appropriate questions	
Diagnostic skills	
Confidentiality	
Contract setting	
Refraining skills	
Self-awareness	
Empathy	
Objectivity	
Referral skills	

CHAPTER 5
A Structure for Listening

Listening is a process

Listening well is difficult and rare for two main reasons. The first is that we get in the way, with our own thoughts and concerns; our own views and feelings; our desire to contribute our bit of the conversation. The second reason is that we don't have a clear structure for listening.

You need to work hard at the first, since it's the most important skill in counselling, and in many other activities. As to the second, I offer a structure here that, if you practise it, will certainly give you a valuable tool.

Listening isn't just one simple process. It demands most of the skills outlined in the previous chapter. It is based on the needs that all of us have, if we are to grow emotionally and intellectually. These needs are:

- To be listened to
- To be heard
- To be understood
- To be accepted and
- To get a response.

Think about these needs for a moment, in relation to your own experience. Make some notes here to show what may happen

A Structure for Listening

if someone is not listened to, heard, understood, accepted and responded to.

_____

_____

_____

To listen: set a contract

In order to listen properly, and to show that you are listening, you need to do some preparation. It's important to make it clear from the start of any interaction, and most of all in counselling, what the nature of the interaction is. In other words, you need to set a contract with the person being counselled.

This is true whether you know the person or not. The contract should include things like where, when and for how long you will be meeting; what you will be offering as a counsellor; what the other person expects and hopes for; what the boundaries are, if any; the issue of confidentiality; the distinction between counselling and any other role you may have; and of course the fact that you will be there to listen, not to manage. There may be a number of other points that need to be agreed between you, perhaps to do with the organisation's structure and policy.

Ensuring that you go through the procedure of setting a contract also sets the scene for listening. The other person is already rehearsing inwardly what he or she wants to say as though you are already listening. You have begun to engender that most essential of qualities for successful counselling — trust.

To hear: identify the issue

You are probably familiar with people who beat about the bush before getting to the point; equally, you probably know people who let them do it. Picture the scene. June goes into the manager's office, wanting 'a word'. The manager chats about the latest work schedule, the weather, asks if everything's all right. 'Fine', says June. 'I just wondered if there was any chance I could alter my shift hours.' They talk about the practicalities, the difficulties, come to a compromise. June is about to leave, when the manager notices her hesitation. 'Is there a problem, June?' 'As a matter of fact, there is. I just can't stand working with Frank again.' And she starts to cry.

This is what I call the 'by the way' or the door-knob syndrome. You have heard it, and perhaps done it, many times. After 20 minutes of talking about apparently unimportant things, the person leaving, hand on door-knob, says 'By the way, I failed that test, so I can't apply for that promotion after all.'

Using your counselling skills means that you will enable the person to identify quite quickly what the problem is. You need to pick up all the signals that the person gives out. Note down here what you think those signals might be. They add up to a message, which is what you have to become aware of.

_____

_____

_____

Check Chapter 7 to compare your ideas with those given in this book.

To understand: clarify what is presented

Once you have identified what it is that is worrying the other person, you can start to understand it, but only if you work hard and concentrate. Understanding what someone else is experiencing comes, not from your own experience, but rather from discovering what is actually being presented to you.

For this, you have to ask for clarification. Sometimes, you need to say or do little, but just indicate that you are waiting for more. The kinds of question you can ask are detailed in Chapter 6. Whatever you do, don't make assumptions and don't jump to conclusions. You are there to help the other person to make sense out of what he or she is saying and feeling and to mirror what is presented to you.

It's always easier to see things clearly when it's not your problem. Your job is to help others to understand things for themselves and to help them take responsibility for it. So getting clarification can be the most crucial part of any counselling session.

To accept: summarise what is being said

You may find yourself counselling someone who has views that you don't agree with. That doesn't matter. People don't have to have the same views. However, in order to counsel people, you do need to accept them as they are, and to accept that what they are saying is, after all, their own experience and belief.

Once someone feels properly accepted, that person is far more likely to be receptive to the counselling process. What you need to do is simply to summarise what it is that you have heard somebody present to you. That doesn't mean that you collude with somebody who displays, for example, a sexist attitude. Your job is to help that person to see it as a problem and get to the root of it.

Unfortunately, it's not all that simple to do and needs some practice. The summary should be succinct, clear and get to the essence of what it is that you have heard.

If you have gone through the previous stages in the structure well enough, you should be able to make a summary that is helpful to both of you. But don't worry if you get something wrong.

The real beauty of giving a summary is that the other person is able to add to it, agree with it, or change it, so that things are clarified even further. In fact the summarising stage can be the one that really takes the person forward in understanding.

To respond: agree appropriate action

By now, the person receiving counselling should be in a position to make some sense out of what he or she has been saying. You have been responding all the way through, of course, but now you are reaching the stage at which you can begin to ask what the person intends to do to change things.

The person's response may be 'to think about it a bit more' or 'I don't really know.' In either event, all you know is that there appears to be more work to do and, if the person wants it, you should suggest that he or she comes for a further session or more. In other words, you are saying that you intend to be available to help this person until he or she resolves the issue. Counselling is seldom a matter of a 'quick fix' solution. You are taking on a commitment.

The structure

To summarise this chapter, the structure for the listening process is as follows:

Process	Structure	Practice
LISTEN	CONTRACT	Where, when, role, rules, purpose, confidentiality ...
HEAR	IDENTIFY	What's presented, signals: the underlying message
UNDERSTAND	CLARIFY	Questions, meanings, connections, discovery
ACCEPT	SUMMARISE	Checking out, playing back, mirroring
RESPOND	ACTION	Encouraging a move forward, next steps

Task

Now is the time to try out some of these things. Practise with someone else (perhaps somebody wanting to do the same) the listening process and structure outlined here. Get some feedback for yourself and note how you do. Then try it again.

CHAPTER 6
Asking Questions

Types of question

There are various questions that you can ask during a counselling session. Getting those questions clear for yourself will help you, not only with your counselling, but also with your interviewing and coaching techniques and the other interpersonal skills that you need as a manager.

The kinds of questions that you will find are most useful are:

- Open
- Closed
- Mirror or reflecting; and
- Probing.

The questions you should avoid are those that are:

- Leading
- Qualified; and
- Multiple.

Open questions

These are questions that require more than a simple answer, demanding that the other person thinks about the response and perhaps answers at some length. The questions will often begin with how or what, such as 'How did you become involved in that?' or 'What kind of work do you enjoy doing?'

Avoid asking questions that begin with 'Why...'. Such questions may appear threatening and discourage an open response from the person. 'Why did you do it that way?' can imply (even if you don't intend it) that you disapprove, causing a defensive response.

Other open questions can start with 'Tell me about...', or 'Would you like to describe what happened?' or 'It would help if I understood more about...'.

Open questions are the most appropriate in the identifying the issue stage described in Chapter 5 (page 43). In other words, you use these kinds of question in order to hear what someone is really saying and to identify the key issue or issues.

Closed questions

There is nothing wrong with closed questions as long as you don't use them too often, otherwise it will become an interrogation session. Closed questions, as you probably know, are ones that require only a simple factual answer. 'Did you know that?', 'How long have you been here?', 'Had you known her before?' are all examples of closed questions.

You can use these in the contract setting stage and in checking things for yourself later on, particularly in the summarising stage. Always take care when using closed questions that you are not closing the person down or leading them to the easy option. Asking 'Do you feel better now?' is probably meant more for you than the other person, so that when you get a 'Yes, thanks' (what else are they going to say?), you're the one who actually feels better.

Mirror or reflecting questions

These are probably the most useful (and underused) types of question. Good counsellors will use a great deal of mirroring questions, usually without the other person even being aware of it.

You will use this type of question during the clarifying stage. Jot down here what you think mirroring or reflecting questions are and give some examples.

_____

_____

_____

It's almost as though you are, literally, holding up a mirror so that the other person can see him or herself more clearly; or more accurately, playing back a tape of what they said. It is partly a brief, interim summary of what you've heard, but it is there in order that the person being counselled is constantly aware of what he or she is presenting.

Notice that I use the term 'presenting' rather than 'saying', since you may need to reflect back not just words, but also feelings that you have picked up. We will explore that more in the next chapter.

A mirror type question may be something like 'I've understood you to say that ... is that right so far?' Even more effectively, you might simply repeat the last few words of what someone has said, in the same way that they have said it. Using the same words in the same tone is a very powerful way of conveying to the other person what he or she is presenting. It takes a lot of practice to do this in a way that is helpful rather than patronising.

Probing questions

Once you have helped the other person to identify the key issues and are in the process of clarifying things, you will have highlighted some areas that need further exploration in order to understand more fully what is going on.

Probing questions take you both further. They may not even be in the form of questions. When it is a question, the most common one will be to ask what something means to the person who said it. 'When you said that you don't enjoy that work, can you say what it means to you?'

Just as likely, you can probe silently. Try simply remaining quiet when someone is talking to you. Listen attentively, showing that you are listening. When the other person finishes, try nodding your head, perhaps giving little more than a grunt of approval or quizzical glance. You may be surprised at the effect as long as you don't overdo it.

Leading questions

A leading question suggests the answer. Don't use it in counselling. It is used in order to manipulate people, and they always know when that is being attempted, just as you would. An example: 'You wouldn't do that, would you?'

Qualified questions

Don't add to your questions by qualifying them. If you don't think that a question is clear enough, it won't help to add explanations. If the other person is taking time to answer, don't interrupt his or her train of thought by asking the question in another way.

Counsellors must respect people enough to know that if something needs explaining, they will ask and if they need time, they should have it.

Multiple questions

When you find yourself asking two or three questions at the same time, you are probably nervous. Stop, take a deep breath and start again.

If you have asked more than one question you will either confuse the other person, or you will get a response only to the one that he or she chooses to answer.

Task

Practice and getting feedback for yourself is the best way of knowing that you ask the right kinds of question in the right way.

Find somebody else whom you can rely on to help you in this way. Ideally, use a tape recorder so that you can listen to the session afterwards and analyse how you did.

Carry out an interview. It might be a counselling session, or it could be on anything that the two of you agree. It might be a continuation of the practice session you had from the previous task. Make a note afterwards of the type of questions you asked and the kind of responses you got. Most important of all, ask the other person how he or she reacted to specific questions and the way you asked them. Listen to the tape and the feedback and practise again the things that need to be improved upon.

CHAPTER 7
Signals and Messages

Non-verbal signals and body language

There have been a few references to signals and messages in the previous chapters. The counsellor must be a good observer and adept at making sense of what is being conveyed.

The signals you get will include the words that are spoken and the way they are said, such as the tone of voice, the emphasis given to certain words or phrases, the things that are repeated, the accompanying eye, hand and body movements.

When you consider all the signals you pick up from what someone conveys, you will recognise that the non-verbal and the body signals tell you far more than the actual words alone.

Exercise

As always, practice is needed to become fully aware of the kinds of signal that people give out when they communicate with you. You probably already know what most of the signals are, but may not use them in a conscious way to make sense of what is being presented.

Next time you are with someone, whether in an informal conversation or perhaps at a meeting, do some conscious observing. Afterwards, make a note of what you have picked up, using the headings given here.

Counselling Your Staff

Key words or phrases	Tone of voice	Non-verbal signs

You might need to do this a few times before you really begin to pick up the essential signals. Once again, it will be helpful for you to share this exercise with somebody else and get some direct feedback.

Making a message from the signals

Here is an edited transcript of what Robert presented during a counselling session. Robert is in his mid-forties, has worked with the company for 15 years, has reached a low to middle grade level of management and is faced with the prospect of change due to a restructuring process within the company.

Robert: I don't know where to start really. (*Silence; Robert shifts in his chair, crosses his legs.*)
Counsellor: Where would you like to start?
Robert: (*Clears his throat, looks down at the floor, then at the counsellor.*) I want to know what's going on and what's going to happen to me.
Counsellor: How do you mean, Robert?
Robert: (*Looks at counsellor with an angry glance.*) Well, I mean, with all the changes going on and the rumours flying about, nobody's told me anything. I suppose I'm just supposed to wait until my redundancy notice is handed out, or they move

Signals and Messages

me to another department. You'd think after all this time, they'd have the courtesy to let me know where I stand. I mean, what am I supposed to do? (*His voice is raised, he folds his arms, leans back in his chair.*)

There are quite a few signals in this short excerpt. Jot down here what you pick up.

_____

_____

_____

The signals allow you to ask some questions, of yourself at first. For example: What or who really makes Robert angry? Why the angry glance at you? What is he saying when he asks what he is *supposed* to do? Who are *they*?

If you ask all these questions you will certainly finish up looking like an interrogator, reinforcing what Robert probably already feels about you as an authority figure. Instead, you must both make some sense of what is going on.

The message is the sum of the signals that Robert is giving you. In this instance, it is something like this.

> *Robert appears to be angry at an anonymous authority and feels unable to control his own destiny.*

Note that you can only say what appears to be the case. You have little information so far (although much more than Robert may realise he has given you) and need to check back with him what he is presenting to you. So, having got this small amount and put together some message, it enables you to ask a key question or make a key comment that will help Robert to clarify things.

Counselling Your Staff

Responding to the message

What would you say at this stage?

_____

_____

_____

I would suggest something like this:

> 'You seem to be pretty angry, Robert. I understand that you have felt left out and are unclear about what you are supposed to do. Can you tell me who is making you so angry?'

The point is (if we're right), that Robert needs help to pin down someone tangible if he can. It is difficult, if not impossible, for someone to deal with a problem if it is vague and unnamed.

In this case, Robert was able to talk about his boss and the anger he felt at being overtaken in the promotion stakes. He saw his boss as distant and evasive, unprepared to discuss the future with Robert or give him any positive opportunities for discussion.

When this became clear, Robert saw that he had to confront his boss and discuss this with him. The outcome was a changed perception. His boss told Robert that he had felt uncomfortable about being promoted above Robert and was unsure whether Robert would welcome being consulted, especially when the boss was unsure about the impact of impending changes. Between the two of them, they agreed to prepare a presentation to the senior management team, describing the effect of current uncertainties and suggesting alternative scenarios for change.

What had happened here was that Robert, perhaps for the first time, was encouraged to take some positive action himself in his own destiny.

I don't want to pretend that this was as easy as it sounds or took place as a result of one session. In fact, the action took place after four sessions, during which Robert explored some of the source of his feelings about authority. It transpired that he had always felt dominated by his parents, who had pushed him into a career he hadn't wanted. He had carried on that feeling of being dominated into his family life, where he always acted passively in any decisions relating to his children, then became angry when they took little notice of him.

What this extract shows is that, if you listen and observe, using the skills described, you are able to ask the questions that will get you, and the person being counselled, to the nub of the problem and towards its eventual resolution.

Task

More practice. This time, again ideally with someone who agrees to work with you on this, try picking up the signals from a real conversation, put together the message you get, and write this down. Then formulate the comment or question that you consider will enable the person to make some sense of what he or she has said.

When you have tried this out, obtain some feedback, either from the person or from your taped playback, or preferably, both.

Write up what took place and what you have learned so far in terms of signals and messages. Also jot down any questions you have at this stage.

CHAPTER 8
A Structure for a Counselling Interview

This chapter will take you through a typical structure or set of steps that you might go through during the process of a counselling session.

Setting the scene

Think carefully about the setting and the atmosphere in which you can engender an open, honest exchange. Take account of the following:

- the room; its privacy and comfort level
- the likelihood of interruptions and how you will handle this
- the seating arrangements
- how you will indicate that you are not acting in an authoritarian way.

Practise sitting at a distance and position where the other person is likely to feel properly attended to without being overawed. Try it out with someone else, both as the counsellor and the person being counselled. These details make all the difference to how quickly and effectively you are able to put people at ease and encourage them to share their problem with you.

A Structure for a Counselling Interview

You need to give a clear indication that you accept and respect the other person and that you regard what he or she has to say as of real importance. Perching on the edge of a desk in an open plan office with a phone ringing will not give that impression.

You must be relaxed, yet attentive, facing the other person, keeping good eye contact, about three feet away in a chair of the same height and kind as the other. Don't sit behind a desk; you need to dispense with as many barriers as possible, and a desk is a physical barrier. Ensure that you will have no interruptions.

Establishing the contract

We have already looked at contract-setting. Once you have set the scene, you must agree between the two of you the purpose and process of the counselling. It is not too early to establish straight away what your role is, what the other person can expect from counselling, what the rules are and the timing, place and frequency of any counselling.

It is also important, right from the start, to show that the other person has an equal responsibility, with you, to take part in the counselling process.

The presenting issue

This is where you begin to identify what it is that the person is there for. What you are seeking is what the person really wants to talk about, not necessarily what he or she starts off with.

The presenting issue may well be something like: 'I haven't been feeling very well recently and the doctor said I should take it easy', whereas the underlying problem emerges as: 'I'm going through a marital crisis and I don't know how to handle it.' This, of course, is arrived at after some skilled listening and questioning from you once you have put together the signals and made sense of them. Now at least, you know what your starting point is.

Observing and reflecting back

You are always in the hands of the other person in terms of what precisely you need to do, when you should do it and how you should do it. Sometimes, you may need to do nothing except to sit there, acting as a sounding board while the other person does all the work.

Have faith in the fact that we are our own best healers. Your job is simply to enable that healing to take place. If you need to do nothing, do just that.

Doing nothing is, of course, never quite that. You will need to be concentrating very hard, and observing just what is being given to you. Where you judge that the other person is finding it difficult to make sense of what he or she is saying, then you need to be reflecting back what you have heard and seen.

This is the mirroring process, as we have explored in Chapter 6. In this case, the reflection is less in the form of questions, but rather in the form of saying back exactly what you understand the person to have said in a simplified and succinct way.

Use your feelings and intuition too. For example, if you feel confused by what someone is saying to you, the chances are that the other person is confused too. So, by saying 'I feel confused', you may help to unlock and clarify the confusion in a startling and straightforward way. It has happened to me many times.

Clarifying the key points

You will have established the 'story' that the other person is presenting to you. You will have gained a picture of the person and what is troubling him or her.

The next part of the process is that of gaining a real understanding. Remember two important points.

- The steps in the counselling process, while distinct in terms of what they are trying to do, should not be seen as separated out or forced. Counselling must not come across

as a series of techniques; it is a highly personal process, aimed at developing as well as helping the other person. So, while you must be aware of the different parts of that process, you must come to them in a natural way, following the lead given to you by the person you are helping.
- The reason for clarifying things is not only that you will understand what the issues are, but that the person with the problem will understand them better too. Understanding the root cause and meaning of a problem is the key to being able to deal with it.

Summarising and closing

You should make the end of the session a clear one. Making your summary, or even more productively, helping the other person to make his or her own summary of what has been said, is the sign for you to begin the closing stage.

You are aiming here to arrive at a point where the other person is clear about what he or she wants and intends to be doing to resolve the problem. This may be a tiny step; perhaps the staff member might go away to observe something that happens and his or her own reaction to it. In such a case, you will have agreed a further session after, say, another week to explore things further.

Actions and outcomes do not need to be tangible. Sometimes they may be aimed at helping the person towards a changed perception of him or herself. Helping someone to achieve greater self-confidence might be one of the most positive, and eventually practical, things you can do in counselling.

The length and frequency of sessions

A counselling session should not be open-ended. The usual time set aside is an hour. It may be shorter, it should seldom be longer. Bear in mind that the other person will be thinking a lot about the session afterwards, so much of the actual work takes place when you are not there.

You also need to pace things so that neither of you becomes overloaded or finds herself going round in circles.

Agree, in your contract-setting, a start and finish time and stick to it. About ten or fifteen minutes before the end of the agreed time, begin to make your overall summary and move towards establishing the next steps for the other person.

You will need to be aware of the amount of time you are able and prepared to give to counselling staff. This will depend upon your own circumstances and priorities. Ideally, you will set aside a specific time slot during the week that you allocate to counselling. This way, people will know when you are available and you will be able to make appointments without going over your scheduled time.

Setting a clear end time and sticking to it is also a way of ensuring that the person who tends to talk at length and repetitively learns to use the time better.

There is a train of thought that says 'when people need counselling, they need it now'. There may be isolated occasions when this is so, but usually, as long as people are given sufficient attention to know that you will be listening to them at an appointed time in the near future, they will be satisfied.

As to frequency, again you must judge this according to your own circumstances and the time available against the demand. Sometimes, one session will be sufficient. Other people with more in-depth problems may need five or six sessions on a weekly basis. Once you find that the time and the nature of the difficulty is more than you can handle, you should suggest to the staff member that he or she seeks specialist counselling support. This is outlined in Chapter 13.

Erica's problem

Erica comes in to see you and asks if you have any time right now, she'd like to discuss a 'bit of a problem' she's having. She looks distressed, wringing her fingers, appears to be holding back tears. You have a meeting to go to in ten minutes. What

A Structure for a Counselling Interview

do you do? Give your responses before reading my suggestions.

_____

_____

_____

(This is based on a real session.) You always need to find a balance between showing that you respect and care for staff and the other demands on your time. In this case, Erica appears in need of something right now. You also have a group of people awaiting your attendance at a meeting. They need to be shown respect too.

Your response could be something like this:

'I can see you are distressed, Erica. I'd like to spend some time with you. Let's make it when I don't have to go off to a meeting. Would you be able to come at eleven tomorrow morning? We can have up to an hour then if you want it and I shall make sure we're not disturbed. Meanwhile, it might help if you think about what you want to say. If you'd like to write something down, so much the better.'

Showing Erica that you have recognised her distress and, while you can't see her now, you want to give her proper attention, will almost certainly be sufficient. Asking her to do some preparation indicates that you are taking it seriously and that Erica will need to do some work. There's a very good chance that before she even comes back to see you, she will have begun the process of resolving her own problem. If, on the other hand, Erica really has a crisis on her hands and needs some immediate help, she will let you know and you have to make a decision based on that.

When Erica returns, she says:

'I really don't know what to say. It seemed clear yesterday, but after I thought about it, things seem even more confused.'

Counselling Your Staff

Your response?

_____

_____

_____

Since this is the start, don't forget the contract-setting stage. Something like this would be appropriate:

> 'Don't worry about feeling confused, Erica; it's probably a good start. My job will be to listen to you and to help you to get things clear. Then, if there's a problem, I'll try to help you to deal with it. Before we start, I just want to say that anything you tell me here will be entirely confidential. The only records I'll keep will be for my own use and I certainly won't discuss what you say with anybody else; unless we agree together that I should do so. I'm not acting as a manager now, but as your counsellor. I've set aside an hour now, so we have plenty of time if we need it. And if there is more to discuss and you want to come back, we shall make another appointment. I've held all calls and the engaged sign is on the door. Is there anything else you'd like to add, or to ask? (*Erica shakes her head and says that seems fine.*) All right then, where would you like to start?'

Erica sits on the edge of her chair, appears uncomfortable, although she smiles at you. She says:

> 'As long as it's confidential. You see, nobody else at work knows this.' (*You nod reassuringly.*) 'I've got a daughter. She's just turned 13; but she's never lived with me. My parents have had custody of her since she was a baby because I couldn't look after her. Now she wants to come and live with me and I want her to, but my parents won't hear of it. It's terrible. There's nothing I can do. It's affecting my work and everything now. Martin (*her supervisor*) keeps telling me off and all I do is cry.' *She starts to cry now.*

A Structure for a Counselling Interview

Your response?

_____

_____

_____

You probably have a lot of questions to ask Erica. How come she couldn't look after her daughter? What's her relationship with her parents and her daughter? Is she alone? Where's the father? Has she spoken to a social worker? And many more. You may even have some advice to give her. You might also have made some assumptions about Erica. At this stage, however, you just need to know, and to let Erica know, that you have heard her properly. So give back to her what you have heard to make sure you and she are talking about the same thing and that you have identified the issue presented to you.

> 'I just want to make sure I've got this right Erica. You have a daughter, now 13, who lives with your parents. Both you and your daughter want her to live with you, but your parents don't want that and this is causing you a lot of distress, including your having a hard time at work with Martin telling you off.'

You'll see that the important thing here is simply to feed back what you have heard, not to come up with interrogative questions or easy solutions. You'll have noticed that Erica not only has a problem with her parents, but also with her supervisor. Maybe there is a connection here. It's too early to jump to conclusions, but you need to store these things in your mind.

Erica says:

'Yes, that's right. You see, I was only 15 when I had Karen. I couldn't stand it at home and wanted to leave as soon as I could, but my parents had adopted Karen as their own. Now she hates it there as well. Now that I've got a good job and my own place I can offer her a home and I'd really love to. She comes to visit at weekends and it breaks me up when she has to go back. I'm sorry to be like this. I really don't know why I'm telling you. You can't do anything. I'm sorry. I'm so useless. I'm sure Martin is going to give me the sack; I keep making stupid mistakes. It's why I thought I'd better come and see you.'

Your response?

___

___

___

Although it may seem as though Erica is rambling on, she is beginning to make sense of things for herself and for you. Now you need to help her to clarify things more so that you can both understand what is going on in preparation for what Erica could do about it.

It is going to be hard for you to help Erica to deal with the situation between her parents and her daughter. This may need some specialist help from someone with more counselling experience. What you can do is to recognise the connection between Erica's feeling of failure with her family and her feelings of failure now in her work, and in particular with her difficulty in relation to her supervisor.

Pointing out the connection, by asking Erica if she can see it herself, can help her to break the perception she has of herself as always being a failure. You need to ask questions that will help her to distance her earlier experience from her current self-perception and behaviour. Erica has become trapped in her lack of self-belief as a young parent of 15, although she is now 28, and she seems to have carried that into her lack of ability to communicate properly with others in authority.

This example is based on a real problem. The outcomes were that 'Erica' realised that her lack of confidence was due to her parents' lack of trust in her, and that she was now able to carry out her work effectively, but found it hard to accept that. She changed two things.

First, she went to speak to 'Martin', her supervisor, asked him for an appraisal session and told him that she had been going through a difficult personal problem and would appreciate his support over the next week or two. In fact, he gave her a high rating and said that he'd been worried about her.

Second, she contacted a mediator in the Family Services Unit, who arranged a meeting between the family. The result was an increase in the access 'Erica' had to her daughter and the virtual transfer over time of the daughter's permanent living arrangements to be with her mother.

The key to the change was in the insight that 'Erica' had once she saw how she was treating herself. She would have been far less likely to take any positive action if she had not accepted personal responsibility. Advising her to talk to her boss, see a social worker and become more confident would probably have reinforced her own low self-esteem. Holding up a mirror to her allowed her to see herself as she was now.

Task

Either: discuss this section and the example with a colleague; or, if you're ready, carry out a counselling session and record the essence of the problem and how you handled the session.

CHAPTER 9
Taking and Keeping Notes

Why take notes?

The issue of records of a counselling session is one that many people raise. It is often seen as a problem, but it doesn't need to be, as long as you are clear about why you are taking notes and what you should do once you have taken them.

The problems are usually put like this:

- If counselling is supposed to be confidential, how can we be seen to be taking notes of what is said?
- How can I concentrate and take notes at the same time?
- How can I remember what has been said if I don't make notes as we go along?
- Should I show the notes to the member of staff being counselled?
- Should anyone else see the records I keep and if so, who and in what circumstances?

With these kinds of question, you may well wonder why you should make and keep any record of anything from the counselling interview. Here are the reasons I give; it is up to you to adapt them to your own situation and follow the appropriate course of action.

> Notes are to aid you in assisting the staff member being counselled. This means that there are two main reasons to keep a record. The first is to act as a reference of the key issues and action raised by the staff member so that you will be able to pick this up at a subsequent session. The second is for your own continued development in counselling, where you record the process you went through and make an assessment of your own performance.

Remember always that the staff member being counselled is your client during this process. That will help you in deciding why you are taking any records and what to put in them. It also means that if, during your contract-setting stage, the staff member wants no record kept at all, his or her wishes must be respected.

When to take notes

When you are counselling, you not only need to be listening and concentrating hard, you also need to show that you are doing this. When the counsellor takes notes during an interview it is almost always counter-productive.

The person being counselled may be put off by the note-taking, wondering what you are writing down, worrying whether, despite your assurances, you will be passing on the notes to an unwanted third party.

The counselling interview is not like a job interview, where the interviewer needs to remember at lot of comparative information. In that case, the interviewer is acting on behalf of the organisation or department. In counselling, you are working in the best interests of the staff member.

It needs practice and confidence to be able to go through a whole counselling session without taking any notes and then to write them up afterwards. But what excellent practice it is. Once you do this a few times you will be amazed at your own ability to recall the main issues raised and to note your own responses made during the interview.

Ideally, you should leave aside time to write up your records directly after the session. If you rush off to a meeting, or have lunch first or make a few phone calls, you will almost certainly find it hard to regain the essence of the counselling session.

What kind of notes to take

First, since confidentiality is essential, make sure that you identify the person only by a code or in some other way so that anyone seeing the record would not know who it was.

Your notes do not have to be long. Essentially, they should include:

- The main issue or issues presented by the staff member
- Your understanding of any underlying problems
- A summary of the stage arrived at during the interview, with any action planned by the staff member and the date of any subsequent counselling session
- A self-assessment of your counselling performance and how you carried out the interview.

Who are the notes for?

The notes that you take are for you, even though their primary aim is better to serve the staff member. This doesn't mean that they are necessarily for your eyes only, dependent upon the circumstances.

Before looking at those circumstances, just a word about notes for the member of staff.

Take another look at the definition of counselling I have given in Chapter 3 (pages 28–29). From this, you will see that a central aim in counselling is for the person being counselled to take responsibility for his or her problem and work towards being able to resolve it.

That being so, it is inappropriate to write up notes to give to the staff member. Instead, and far more relevant to your purpose, always ask the people you counsel to write up their own notes, especially the things that they have discovered about themselves and any action they intend to take. The staff member can write those notes during your session, or perhaps do them as part of the action to bring back, the next time. Those notes will be, after all, the most significant ones, since the person will be taking personal responsibility for them.

Returning to who your notes are for; they may be for you to share with the member of staff and they are certainly for you to read before your next session with the same person. They may also be shown to the person acting as your counselling supervisor (see Chapter 12).

In this last case, it is essential that you discuss this beforehand with the staff member and explain the purpose (for your own training and development) and the role of the supervisor. It will also be obvious at that point that your counselling supervisor must be somebody completely separate from the staff member and certainly not having any line management capacity over him or her.

If you do have a supervisor, that person will almost certainly guide you as to the most helpful kind of notes for you to take.

The other person who might see the notes is anyone who takes on the role of counselling the staff member in your place, for whatever reason. Again, this must be with the agreement of the staff member, who should always be kept fully consulted about the status of any records.

How and where to keep records

Clearly, somewhere secure in a form that makes the record inaccessible to anyone else. The last place to keep counselling notes is in the staff member's own employment file. If your record is on a computer, take special care to ensure its security.

You should have a separate counselling file, using codes so that only you can identify the person.

Counselling Your Staff

Task

If you don't already have a satisfactory one, devise a system for keeping secure recordings of your counselling sessions. Then, using a practice session with a colleague, or on a training course (perhaps one you've done already while working with this book) make some notes of that session and share them with your colleague and/or tutor.

_____
_____
_____
_____
_____

CHAPTER 10
Who Should Be the Counsellor?

The manager?

It is common within organisations for the line manager to adopt the role of counsellor with his or her member of staff. This can lead to a number of difficulties as you will have realised. Line managers who offer counselling do so usually in an informal way.

In other words, they will seldom establish a proper understanding or contract, they are unlikely to offer a continuing opportunity to the member of staff and they may never even indicate that they are providing counselling.

That is not to say that the skills of counselling are not a valuable and important tool for any manager, used in an informal way. What it does mean is that the manager who does any counselling must be fully aware of the implications of taking that road.

What do you consider to be some of the advantages and disadvantages of the line manager as counsellor? How would you deal with them?

Counselling Your Staff

Advantages	Disadvantages	My action

You are in a particularly delicate position when attempting to counsel a member of your own staff. You need to be specially clear, first with yourself, about your role as a counsellor as distinct from your role as the person's manager.

Suppose, for example, that the person's problem is to do with another member of your staff, or another manager, or even yourself? Perhaps the problem is one that you find distasteful. This could easily prejudice your ability to deal with the member of staff, not so much as a counsellor, but as the manager.

Someone not in a direct managerial position?

Many companies have a pool of managers who become able and willing to take on the role of counsellor for members of staff for whom they do not have direct managerial responsibility.

Apart from the advantages this has in terms of not crossing boundaries and the maintaining of confidentiality, it becomes easier for the member of staff to open up to someone when the fear of management reprisal doesn't add to the difficulties already facing the person. There is another advantage too.

The organisation that encourages managers to take on the skills of counselling and to practise this within their work with other members of staff, is potentially a healthier organisation in terms of its human resources.

Who Should be the Counsellor?

How would you go about encouraging and assisting this approach within your own organisation?

_____

_____

_____

Someone designated as a counsellor?

A third approach is for the organisation to invite, train and designate people to take on a counselling role as a part of their work, regardless of their other designations or managerial responsibilities. This was described in Chapter 1. When members of staff are in need of counselling support, they can have access to a person, perhaps within their own department, who is not their manager and who is seen as objective and having only a counselling role with the employee.

What do you consider to be the advantages and disadvantages of this system?

Advantages	Disadvantages

Counselling Your Staff

Task

Map out what you consider to be the most appropriate way for your organisation to offer counselling. How would you go about setting up and/or maintaining this programme?

_____
_____
_____
_____
_____
_____
_____
_____
_____

CHAPTER 11
Training for the Counsellor

Resources

Training programmes and courses for counselling can be found in a range of places and formats. You could go on a three-day or a three-year course, depending on your own interest and readiness. You can learn through books, through distance learning programmes, through evening courses, through individual or group sessions or through becoming involved in one of the counselling organisations scattered throughout the country.

A quick scan of your local or national newspaper will give you an idea of the range of counselling programmes available. A visit to the library and a perusal of the leaflets and other literature available will give you more information.

Contacting some of the national organisations, or their local branches, will give you further knowledge of the extent and range of the services and the training available. The British Association for Counselling, based in Rugby, has useful material and a network of members, many of whom are registered to offer training within organisations.

It will be an investment, for you and for your organisation, for you to take up some training in counselling skills if you are contemplating carrying out this role in the workplace. Often the best way to discover whether or not you want to get involved in counselling is to go on a short training course as a taster. Many people who do so find that they have developed their skills significantly and become hungry for more.

Investigate some of the possibilities and resources local to you and jot them down here.

Organisation	Address	Phone/Contact

Practice and experience

Whatever the training, there is never any real substitute for practice. Much of the point of any training is that you will normally get to practise some counselling in a supportive and tutored environment. In fact, you should investigate any course before you take it on to ensure that you will get some good 'hands on' experience.

The newer you are to counselling, the more practice you need to get. It can be quite nerve-racking carrying out your first counselling session. If your first practice is on a member of staff who comes to you with a problem, your nervousness can create more tension than he or she started out with.

Ideally, you should get this practice during a training programme. An excellent substitute for this is to practise with a colleague and to carry out what is called 'co-counselling'. In co-counselling, the two of you take it in turns to counsel the other person and then to give and receive some feedback from the process.

Even more effective than this is the triad. Here you work with two other people. One acts as an observer and tutor, another does the counselling, while the third is the 'client'. The roles are exchanged so that each of the three of you carries out all three in turn. Working in this way is one of the most valuable (as well as cost-effective) training processes. The essential thing is to use a disciplined approach and to ensure that you go through the processes described in this book.

Note down here who you could work with in this way and, when you have discussed it with them, arrange some practice sessions.

Who I could work with	When we'll meet
1.	
2.	
3.	
4.	
5.	

Once you have had some training, absorbed the key points made in this book and taken up some opportunities for practice, you'll need to do some counselling. Getting this real experience is the best training of all, as long as you continue to learn from the process.

This is where the importance of keeping adequate and relevant records will become obvious. Maintaining records for your own increasing competence and skills in counselling, will not only enhance the counselling work you do with staff but will greatly enhance your own understanding of people and communication in general. Even after 20 years of counselling, I find that I continually learn from the people who come to see me and the way I have responded. In the early stages of your counselling, you will have a steep learning curve and you can be your own best teacher if you take it seriously.

Getting feedback

The processes described above will give you the feedback essential to your being able to develop your skills. In addition, you will need to get some information about the efficacy of your counselling. More of this is included in Chapter 17.

Part of the feedback you can get will be from the members of staff whom you counsel. In order to get this, you could leave aside a part of the time at the end of a session to ask the person being counselled for some feedback. This moves the focus away from the member of staff, and could have either a positive or negative effect. You will have to judge that for yourself in the particular circumstances.

The other thing you can do is to ask the staff member to take away a brief questionnaire and to let you have this back after a day or two. This can have the triple effect of establishing some follow-up contact, of having the member of staff think about the issue he or she has discussed with you and of giving you some feedback. It also indicates that counselling is a process that provides staff with a thoughtful and professional service intended.

Here is an example of a questionnaire that you could use. Adapt it for your own circumstances.

Counselling feedback form	Comments
How satisfied were you with the way counselling was explained to you?	
Describe how you felt listened to and understood.	
What did you think of the way your counsellor communicated with you?	

How far do you feel that you were able to discuss your problem?	
What can you say about the progress you made during the session?	
What did you like about the counselling?	
What did you dislike about the counselling?	

Task

Devise a training and feedback programme for yourself, based on your own needs and interests and the resources and opportunities available to you.

_____

_____

_____

_____

_____

_____

_____

_____

_____

CHAPTER 12
Supervision and Support

Counselling can be lonely

Not only is counselling carried out by one person working with another in need of support, but its nature means that you cannot easily talk to someone else about it. The need to keep things confidential means that you are not at liberty to go to a colleague at work, or home to your partner and say, 'You'll never guess what I heard today.'

Without any feedback, and even with it, it is hard to know how you are doing and whether you are having any effect and are improving your skills.

One of the requirements of an accredited counsellor, certainly one in membership of organisations like The British Association for Counselling or Relate, is that he or she has a supervisor, or person who acts as a tutor and support on a regular basis. This is as true of people with years of experience as it is of people in training.

From this, you will see the recognition given to the need for people who carry out counselling to receive consistent support themselves from somebody fully conversant with the process.

For the person carrying out the counselling of staff within the work environment, it may be difficult to gain the kind of support necessary; first because it may not be recognised as needed (and therefore the resources not provided), and second because it may be hard to find a supervisor.

Carrying other people's burdens

One of the real benefits for people in going to see a counsellor is that they can dump their problems. Just talking about something that feels insoluble and depressing can be sufficient to lighten the person's load.

The difficulty for you doing the counselling is that the load can be dumped on you! If you are not very careful, after a few counselling sessions dealing with people's problems, the world can appear like one big problem and you are carrying most of it around.

This is why professional counsellors seek support for themselves.

Even if you feel quite confident and able to dismiss from your thoughts and emotions the problems of other people, you must be fully aware of the implications of listening to those problems on a regular basis. The difficulty is that one person's specific problem may well resonate with some, possibly painful, experience that you have had yourself. If that is so (and it's more common than you might imagine) you will find it hard to deal with the other person. Instead, you will be thinking about your own experience. When your staff member goes away, you'll be left with his or her problem to think about, and revived memories of your own.

Having a supervisor to help you to review your counselling will turn that potentially negative experience into a positive and learning one for you.

Finding support

List the possible sources of support that you could find for yourself. Note how you would go about setting up that support.

_____

_____

_____

_____

You might have included colleagues at work; your own manager; somebody outside your organisation involved in counselling; a member of a counselling training course; a professional counsellor; someone recommended to you by a counselling agency.

Now note down what you would seek from that person.

_____

_____

_____

What counselling supervision is; where to find it

Supervision, in the counselling sense, is a process whereby the counsellor is helped to explore the practice of counselling as he or she is carrying it out.

The supervisor will be somebody experienced and adept at counselling and also at providing supervision. He or she will probably be someone who carries out training in counselling. Part of counselling supervision will be, in fact, training.

The counsellor will need to discuss the counselling that he or she has undertaken. This brings up the issue of confidentiality. While specific names may not be used, it is always possible that the circumstances would identify an individual. It is essential, therefore, that you discuss this both with the staff member seeing you for counselling and the supervisor beforehand.

The contract of confidentiality with the member of staff should include your request to discuss in confidence the counselling session with your tutor or supervisor with a view to assisting you with your own practice. The supervisor will also be bound by the code of confidentiality that you agree.

Good counselling supervisors are not easy to find and will usually expect payment. The same sources of information that you found for counselling courses will serve for the search of a supervisor.

Supervision and Support

You will need to be aware that there are many different counselling approaches and specialisms. In the kind of counselling you are likely to be doing, you will probably find it useful to find a counsellor who uses a 'client-centred' approach and who has some experience with counselling in the workplace. Don't imagine that you have to use the first supervisor who comes along. Just as your own staff should have a choice in who counsels them, you should exercise choice in who suits you best as a supervisor.

At the very least, if you have difficulty in obtaining proper supervision, work with one or two other people from inside or outside your organisation, in a similar way to that described in Chapter 11, to gain support for your counselling.

Task

Discuss the topic of support and supervision with others in your organisation. Make some enquiries to investigate possible sources for supervision and the comparative costs involved. Write down how you will go about establishing adequate support and supervision for yourself.

_____

_____

_____

_____

_____

CHAPTER 13
Counselling Issues and Situations

In your counselling, as long as you are open-minded (a vital characteristic for a counsellor), you will find yourself confronted by a variety of issues. They are all natural human experiences and events. In the normal course of a day, you are unlikely to be aware of them all around you. When you sit with someone long enough to listen to what he or she has to say, you will discover an apparently extraordinary array of concerns.

Here are some of the issues that you can find in counselling people:

- Relationships (personal and work)
- Employment problems
- Marital problems
- Bereavement and loss
- Trauma
- Family difficulties (children, parents, partners)
- Alcohol and drug misuse
- Health concerns (such as cancer, AIDS, etc).

You are not expected to be an expert in all, or in any of these issues. You may have experienced problems in some of them yourself, or have some knowledge of a particular area. There may even be a disadvantage in having specific knowledge; the temptation there may be to offer advice instead of just listening and trying to understand what the person is experiencing so that you can help him or her to deal with it.

There are two main things for you to do. The first, as always, is to go through the listening and counselling process described in this book. The second is to have information about the agencies local to you who are able to offer specialist assistance if this is required by your member of staff. As long as you know the area of concern, and as long as the staff member has identified a desire to seek such help, you should pass on the relevant information. This is when advice, in the form of information, is appropriate.

Here is an example of a counselling problem.

A drink problem

> Hugh comes to see you. He tells you that his boss has suggested he talks to you. Eventually Hugh gets around to telling you that he has a drink problem that is becoming noticeable at work. He also confides in you that his wife has threatened to leave him. He says that he has been drinking on and off for nearly seven years, but he never saw it as a problem. Now he thinks he must do something but isn't sure he could face Alcoholics Anonymous.

Of course there is much more; there usually is with someone who needs to resort to such 'escape routes' as drinking heavily. You already know that Hugh has marital problems, and probably work ones too. There are no doubt several things at the root of Hugh's problem. The fact that he has come to you (even if his boss suggested it) indicates that Hugh is taking things seriously, perhaps for the first time.

He has expressed diffidence about going to Alcoholics Anonymous. What you need to do is to explore with him what makes that difficult. Once you have established that, you may be able to offer Hugh sufficient assistance for him to take the (always difficult) first step to joining AA or another similar organisation.

If Hugh is an alcoholic, you are probably not equipped to help him to stop drinking; that requires specialised skill and the support of others in the same situation. What you can do is to support Hugh sufficiently for him to seek that specialist help.

Having the name and phone number of an individual from a specialist organisation is of immense help to anyone seeking that support. You need to compile a list and, most important, keep it up to date by checking on a regular basis.

Relationships (personal and work)

Most problems are, in some way, to do with relationships. In turn, most relationship problems stem from past difficulties, perhaps a childhood trauma or negative experience.

For example, a staff member who has a problem with a colleague may be seeing that person as having the same traits as someone he or she knew and disliked in the past. Sometimes, simply asking if this person is a reminder of someone else is enough to trigger an insight.

Such things are often deep-seated and difficult to reach. You may have neither the time nor the knowledge to deal with really difficult and potentially destructive relationship issues. In these cases, you would do well to encourage the person to see a professional counsellor. The work you do might be the starting point for the member of staff who needs more in-depth counselling than you are likely to be able to offer. This doesn't make what you do less valuable; in fact you are providing the first opportunity for the person's continuing development.

Employment problems

These may be the most common of all issues that you find walking into your counselling sessions. Frequently, such problems are to do with impending and current changes within the organisation. Changes of all kinds, especially when imposed rather than in the control of the individual, can cause a great deal of distress.

Such changes might include redundancy, redeployment, promotion; or less apparently major changes such as new technology, moving offices or any other alteration in the usual way someone functions in his or her employment.

Don't forget that you are offering counselling. It is easy for the staff member to see you as the representative of an organisation imposing the hated change and to express anger directly at you. Your role is not to defend or to justify or to explain the changes, but to offer the staff member the chance to express that anger and to decide how he or she is to handle the change productively.

Specialist agencies exist to offer counselling (and advice) on redundancy, new careers, retraining and so on.

Other employment issues may have to do with frustration and disappointment, perhaps to do with lack of career advancement or aborted projects. The counsellor must be careful to separate the organisational aspects from the personal ones. You can help the staff member to look at their personal feelings; you can't change the way the organisation operates (although see Chapter 17).

Issues that may well need to be drawn more directly to the attention of managers in the organisation are to do with harassment at work, a breakdown in your equal opportunities policy, or other events which are illegal or against company policy. Even here, you are bound to maintain confidentiality. It is up to the staff member to carry forward any action, while your role is to support them through the counselling process. If they ask for your help directly, you must be quite clear with the person what you are prepared to do and where this conflicts with your counselling function. The referral here may be to another manager within the organisation.

Marital problems

Most marital problems are best dealt with by seeing the two people involved. This, again, is a specialist skill. Your contribution will be to work within your own ability, probably listening as always, providing the background support for someone going through a difficult period and perhaps supporting him or her in seeing a counsellor at your local Relate.

Relate, incidentally, has an exceptionally good range of books on counselling available from its bookshop in Rugby, as well as intensive training for marriage and relationship counsellors.

Bereavement and loss

Bereavement organisations, like Cruse, know that people go through phases after the death of someone close. There is grief, of course; but also bewilderment, anger, guilt and similar, sometimes unexpected emotions are there. It is also common for people who have been bereaved to find themselves avoided by others after the first few weeks, while they continue to mourn for a year or often much longer.

Allowing a bereaved person to express his or her emotions in a counselling session, and letting them know that it's quite normal to feel those things, can be the most helpful thing anyone can do.

Trauma

The cases of trauma that you are most likely to deal with are probably through work-related events. Such events may be accidents, whether experienced directly or witnessed, or some other sudden shock.

> Martin is a train driver. Last week a woman jumped in front of his InterCity express. He comes to see you, still shocked from the incident, not sure whether he can ever drive a train again. 'I never had a chance', he says. 'If only I'd seen her maybe I could have sounded my signal and she'd have stepped back.'

Usually, people just need to talk about these kinds of experience to get over their shock and feelings of guilt. In the past, organisations have been poor at recognising the support that people need in order to regain their confidence and ability to function effectively after having gone through trauma of this nature.

Specialist counsellors, dealing with the after effects of personal trauma (usually taking place in childhood), are best at helping people who need more than the listening ear.

Family difficulties (children, parents, partners)

Sometimes the only place for people to talk about their family problems is at work. This goes on naturally between colleagues and is part of the social importance of working life.

But where the issue becomes overwhelming to the extent that it affects people's work, the counsellor has a valuable function, supporting the person with the problem and relieving other staff members of a burden.

Once again, you can offer counselling within your own boundaries, after which you could suggest other specialist help. Youth organisations can assist in helping parents with 'problem' children, there are family counselling agencies and some of the statutory agencies, like social services and probation departments offer counselling and conciliation work.

Alcohol and drug misuse

This is a difficult area and every effort should be made to get people to seek help from an appropriate organisation. You have an important role in acting as a kind of bridging help, providing the support and impetus to members of staff to take further steps towards dealing with their problems.

Health concerns (such as cancer, AIDS etc)

There is a considerable amount of fear and ignorance about a variety of illnesses and how they affect people. Obviously, people concerned about their own health need to take medical advice.

Apart from that, as a person offering counselling within your organisation, you need to be as informed and open-minded as you can be. Most important of all, you need to show acceptance of the person and his or her concerns. The issue may include problems the person is having with other members of staff or family because of concern about their health.

Where the issue is AIDS, there could be a great deal of prejudice and abuse of the person. It is vital that you don't add to that, even inadvertently, by believing some of the misconceptions about the disease. You have a responsibility to make yourself as informed as possible before attempting any counselling. Pick up the latest information on AIDS from your library or health centre and familiarise yourself with it. And do talk to someone from one of the AIDS organisations (see Appendix).

The same is true of other illnesses, whether they are mental or physical. Almost everyone is ill at some time. Your job as a counsellor is to help people where they need support at work. Part of the outcome may well be that the incidence of illness is reduced; or at least that a person's ability to work effectively is not marred by health problems.

Task

Find out and record information on specialist agencies in your area.

Counselling Issues and Situations

Issue	Agency/Phone No	Contact person
Relationship		
Employment		
Marital		
Bereavement		
Trauma		
Family		
Alcohol/Drug abuse		
Health/AIDS		
Other		

CHAPTER 14
A Code of Practice for Counselling

Activity

To begin with, consider the following statements. Discuss them with someone else if you can. Make a few notes.

1. The counsellor's goal is to make people better adjusted to society.

2. The counsellor should be in control of the interview at all times.

3. If the person talks about a number of problems at the same time, you should tell him or her to concentrate on one at a time.

4. If the person presents a point of view that is obviously prejudiced the counsellor should put him or her right.

A Code of Practice for Counselling

5. It is rarely helpful for the counsellor to be directive in giving solutions.

6. The counsellor should give advice when the person requests it.

7. If the counsellor feels the person is persisting in wasting time, he or she should say so.

8. The counsellor should allow the person to make self-critical statements.

9. After the working relationship has been established the counsellor should begin to interpret the person's unconscious attitudes and feelings.

10. The counsellor should communicate negative feelings (eg anger) that he or she may feel towards the person.

11. The counsellor should have only a limited expectation of change in a person's behaviour.

12. The counsellor should at all times be silent about his or her own personal experiences when counselling.

___

___

You won't find my responses here; your own are the important ones.

Exercise

Now write down a paragraph saying what your reasons and values are in offering to counsel other people.

___

___

___

___

___

I hope that you have completed this exercise; it's probably the most important one in the book. No matter what skills you will have picked up along the way, your counselling will be informed primarily by your values and beliefs. I don't offer a 'model set' of values, they will have been apparent throughout the book. Here are some ideas:

- People are best able to resolve their own issues when listened to.
- Counselling helps to create an environment of development.
- Counselling enables people to function healthily.
- The organisation benefits from offering counselling to staff.
- Anyone, regardless of background, status, race, religion, gender or sexual orientation, should have equal opportunity to express his or her feelings and concerns through counselling.

You may like to refer back to Chapter 3 to review your statements and those of my own about the purpose of counselling.

A code of practice

You will have built up a code of practice through the process of establishing a contract in previous sections. This, together with your value statements, will help you to recognise some of the 'rules' you need to follow. Again, there is no model code (although organisations like the British Association for Counselling have an established code of ethics for all of its members). You may need to define your own, to relate to your and the organisation's circumstances.

Some of the issues to consider are confidentiality, relationships, giving advice and initiating the counselling process.

Confidentiality

What boundaries do you have? Suppose someone comes to you confessing to stealing company documents; or a colleague's handbag. How do you handle it? Perhaps a staff member in charge of people's safety (a bus driver for example) tells you he has a drink problem. What do you do?

Relationships

The counsellor is in a potentially very powerful position, certainly in terms of trust. An abuse of the counsellor/staff relationship can totally undermine any good that might have been done.

How do you handle a suggestion from a staff member whom you have been counselling that you go out for lunch? How will you deal with a person who is sexually attractive to you? How do you react when a person starts to cry, especially if they are of the opposite sex to you?

These are all real dilemmas faced by the counsellor. You must be very clear about your boundaries. Knowing them beforehand will be of immeasurable value.

Giving advice

It will often feel much easier to give advice than to take the person through the, often painful, process of self-discovery. You may regularly feel that you have more knowledge, experience and wisdom than the other person, and this may be reinforced by his or her reaction to you. How do you handle that?

Consider the implications of giving advice. Make a decision based on the person's real need and your overall values and beliefs, on when you do and when you don't give advice. If you have even a suspicion that it's the easy way out and it makes you seem more clever, then don't.

There may be times when it is appropriate to give advice. This will nearly always be information that will be helpful to the staff member in his or her quest to resolve a problem. Passing on information about other agencies, for example, is helpful; but even then only after you have established that this is what the person is really seeking and would find helpful.

How do you handle it when the person asks you directly for advice on sorting out a difficult relationship? It may be very tempting to respond by making a suggestion based on your years of greater wisdom and experience. But unless you plan to become an 'agony columnist' for your local newspaper, giving trite responses to people's personal dilemmas, I suggest you hold the good advice.

Initiating the counselling process

In the workplace, it can be common for people to 'be sent' for counselling, as though it's part of a disciplinary process, or a substitute for good management.

As the counsellor, you need to be aware whose problem you are really looking at. Similarly, once you have a counselling role, you may be tempted to suggest to people that they need counselling.

Ideally, people volunteer themselves. It is the first and important step in self-help. It is also a difficult step for people to take.

A Code of Practice for Counselling

You may have to do quite a bit of educative work with managers and others around your organisation so that counselling is recognised as being open to everyone and that it is an acceptable way for people to come and discuss their problems or concerns in confidence.

How do you deal with the manager who asks you to 'have a word' with a member of his or her staff? What do you say to someone who obviously doesn't want to be in your office?

Task

Define a counselling code of practice for yourself. Discuss it with key people in your organisation.

_____

_____

_____

_____

_____

CHAPTER 15
Setting Up a Counselling Programme

Considerations

In using this book (rather than just reading it) you will have added to your skills, knowledge and understanding of counselling your staff. If you are, or intend to be, counselling your own staff as their manager, you will have become aware of the inherent pitfalls.

You may still be in a situation where there is no policy of counselling and find yourself offering it as part of your normal managerial responsibility and natural concern. In that case, knowing the pitfalls will make it easier for you to avoid them.

If a counselling policy and programme does not currently exist in your organisation, you may want to encourage the organisation to set one up. You'll need to consider:

- who you should talk to
- the arguments for developing a counselling programme
- how to recruit people to carry out the counselling
- resources that will be needed and where they can be found
- training and support needs for counsellors.

Guidelines to all those considerations will be found elsewhere throughout this book.

A plan

Armed with ideas from the things you have just considered, draw up a plan to help in the development of a counselling service within your organisation. This might be a new programme, in which case you may want to start with a section, a department or a profit centre; something manageable and capable of being evaluated in, say, a one-year period. If there is already a counselling service, you might want to suggest ways of enhancing it.

Sketch out your plan here.

_____

_____

_____

_____

_____

_____

_____

_____

_____

Try your ideas out on two or three colleagues, preferably people who will have a say in the establishment or development of an internal counselling service. Once you have had their feedback you can hone your plan and decide how, when and where to take it forward. Meanwhile, it doesn't stop you from carrying out any counselling within your own ambit.

Keeping records

There are three main reasons for keeping records, bearing in mind the confidential nature of counselling.

The first two have already been discussed in Chapter 9; that is the development of your own counselling skills and the maintenance of a confidential recording of the main issues the staff member has brought to a counselling session for your ease of follow-up.

A third reason is for the development of the organisation itself, or at least a part of it. Once again, while you must maintain confidentiality, it is an important part of your role to report back at the appropriate level where you have seen clear trends. For example, if you find that you have seen a significant number of people over the previous six months who are experiencing problems coping with a new work system, you are in a position to point it out. If you have discovered an increase in the number of people from one department who are feeling very frustrated, you have evidence of numbers, if not of the specific individuals, who have expressed this.

Don't forget that the counsellor is in a privileged position, hearing much of what goes on. While this is confidential, if a pattern emerges, then the problems presented may be more to do with the running of the organisation (or a part of it) than with the staff members who come to see you.

Evaluating the programme

This brings us to the process of evaluation, on which we will have more to say in Chapter 17. For now, make sure that you include in your plan what and how you will evaluate the success of your counselling, whether this is just you doing it, whether it is a new, pilot programme you are engaged in, or whether it is a continuing large scale service offered by your organisation.

Whatever the case, it is clear that you need to maintain some kind of records to enable you to know how you are doing.

CHAPTER 16
Open for Business!

What to say

You're almost ready to offer counselling. How do you go about telling people?

Whether you will be counselling staff who are directly managed by you or not, it is a good idea to demonstrate that this is being offered as a service rather than as a management edict. It must be seen as different from an appraisal interview, or a coaching discussion or certainly a disciplinary interview.

Indicate the entirely voluntary nature of the service, say something about the nature of counselling (there will be many, sometimes negative, preconceived ideas about it). You have, somehow, to dispel the common myth that you have to be either a weak failure or mentally ill to see a counsellor.

Try to get across the message that counselling is simply an opportunity for people to talk confidentially about anything that is bothering them, and that the service is offered as part of what any caring organisation would do for its staff. You could also emphasise the positive, developmental nature of the process. You will want to use words that convey the message, bearing in mind your type of organisation and the staff who work there.

Write down an outline here that will serve as a poster, leaflet or letter to staff.

Counselling Your Staff

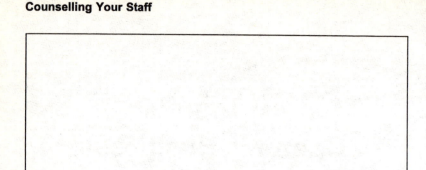

Show it to a few people to get their response.

Where to offer counselling

All the planning and counselling skills you have will go to waste if there is no satisfactory place to use as a counselling room. Quiet rooms are often at a premium in many offices.

Your own office, if you have one, might be good, but can you ensure that you won't get any interruptions? And, especially if you are the line manager, your office may well be an intimidating factor, incongruent with the message you have conveyed that counselling is not being used by management against its staff. Obviously, you have to use your judgement here as well as being realistic about the facilities at your disposal.

The best place is a neutral, quiet, private office, where you can have two chairs, away from a desk and perhaps a low table, so that you can sit at a forty-five degree angle to the other person rather than your facing opposite each other.

Being patient

Patience is essential for anyone doing counselling. This is true when you are working with an individual who may seem to you to take an inordinately long time to accept that a change is needed, never mind to take the action towards that change.

It is even more true when offering counselling for the first time. Nobody seems to come. Then, when they do start to knock on your door, it is just a trickle at first. Despite the fact

Open for Business!

that you may know there is a big need for the counselling you can offer, it is unlikely that people will come flooding in.

This is probably just as well. You need the time and space to get it right. Too many people at first would mean that you could get overwhelmed.

It will take time for staff to trust that counselling can be of help and that there is no stigma attached to it, especially if it has not been offered before. Once you can create a climate of trust and positive support, you and what you have to offer will be accepted and then taken up. But don't be surprised if it takes weeks, even months, before you can really see any sizeable take-up. If you plan for this, you will not be disappointed. Use the time to practise.

If you have set aside a particular time during the week, say every Wednesday at noon, you can use that time to develop your counselling skills even when you have no staff member to counsel. None of that time will go to waste. Don't forget that the skills you have learnt will be useful to you in any contact you have with people, whether in meetings or in negotiation with others.

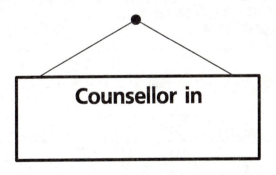

CHAPTER 17
Evaluating the Counselling Programme

Defining your aim

As with any other activity, you can evaluate the success of counselling by being clear at the outset what your goals are and having measurable and realistic targets.

Go back to the beginning, especially Chapter 2, to revisit some objectives that you might have. Think again about your overall goals and those of the organisation. They may be different, although they should not be in conflict with each other.

What are your personal aims? Write them down here.

_____

_____

_____

Now write down some key organisational objectives for counselling.

Objective (quantify)	To be achieved by

For example, an organisational goal might be to reduce staff absenteeism by 15 per cent over the next 12 months.

How to measure success

Once you have established your targets, set up the counselling programme and developed a method of recording that will keep individual files confidential, you should review the process on a regular basis.

Ideally, you will have a number of colleagues, some involved in the counselling, some who are there with decision-taking authority, who will act as a management group for the programme, to include its monitoring and evaluation.

This brings in other aspects of the organisation; certainly its human resources department, probably its finance section, undoubtedly its operations side and hopefully someone from senior management. They will all need to be engaged in some way in the evaluation, looking at such statistics as staff turnover.

This will also be the group that can potentially make changes to respond to needs that have been highlighted through the counselling programme. This means that counselling is not just a long-term development process for the individual, but also for the organisation. It also means that staff can have an impact on the organisation rather than the other way round only.

Counselling Your Staff

Of course, success in counselling will not just be measured through quantitative data extracted from employment records. It is also to be measured through qualitative changes.

These are harder to define and to measure. They will include a greater sense of personal satisfaction at work; individuals who feel better about themselves; improved working relationships; healthier communication; less frustration.

These things can be measured through questionnaires or sample interviews. More likely they will be noticed over a period of time. Practically, they will be seen in a higher and more consistent quality of service provided by staff to each other and to their customers.

CHAPTER 18
A Checklist

Key points to remember

- Know yourself; your strengths and weaknesses.
- Understand your role in counselling.
- Know the benefits of counselling to your organisation.
- Be able to define counselling.
- Have a grasp of the skills needed in counselling.
- Practise those skills.
- Know and practise the listening process and structure.
- Use appropriate questions; be able to distinguish different kinds of questions.
- Learn to pick up the signals that people give out.
- Be able to make an accurate summary to capture the essence of what is presented to you.
- Be able to structure a counselling interview.
- Agree who carries out counselling; for example, line manager or other.
- Get some training in counselling.
- Request feedback for yourself.
- Get support and supervision for your counselling work.
- Inform yourself about the relevant agencies offering specialist help.
- Develop your values and a code of practice.
- Plan your counselling programme (personal and organisational).

Counselling Your Staff

- Organise the recording; ensuring confidentiality.
- Know how to start.
- Be patient.
- Know how to measure counselling success and what to measure.

Task

This is an open-ended task. Record your own thoughts here. You might want to make comments about this book, what you found useful and what you didn't. You may want to review your own ideas about counselling. You could revisit what you think your strengths and weaknesses are in relation to counselling. You could use the space to note what your next steps are.

_____
_____
_____
_____
_____
_____
_____
_____
_____

Finally

I hope that you do develop your interests and abilities and use them in counselling staff. If you do, you will discover that there is nothing final in counselling. You will almost certainly discover, as I have over the past 20 years, that the world becomes a more fascinating and worthwhile place and that you

A Checklist

have something important to offer to other people.

More important, you will learn, and continually learn, about yourself and about others. You will develop considerable powers of observation and insight.

You will also be providing support to people who need it and whose desire is to learn and develop. At the same time you will have an invaluable part to play in the human side of your organisation's development.

Good luck, and good counselling.

Appendix

Further reading

Atkinson, Jacqueline M, *Coping With Stress at Work*, Thorson 1994
Egan, Gerard, *The Skilled Helper: a systematic approach to effective helping*, 5th edition, Brooks/Cole, 1993
Jung, Carl, *The Undiscovered Self: answers to questions raised by the present world crisis*, Routledge, 1974
Munro, EA, Mathei, RJ and Small, JJ, *Counselling: the skills of problem solving*, revised edition, Methuen, 1989
Nelson-Jones, Richard, *Practical Counselling Skills: help clients to help themselves*, Cassell, 1988
Redman, Warren, *Achieving Personal Success: an introduction to inner balancing*, Merlin Star, 1995
Rogers, Carl R, *A Way of Being*, Houghton Mifflin, 1980
On Becoming a Person: a therapist's view of psychotherapy, Constable, 1986
Rowe, Dorothy, *The Successful Self*, Fontana, 1989

Some national referral agencies

British Association for Counselling
1 Regent Place,
Rugby CV21 2PJ
Tel; 01788 578328

CRUSE (Bereavement Counselling)
126 Sheen Road,
Richmond,
Surrey TW9 1UR

The Lighthouse (AIDS Counselling)
c/o 178 Lancaster Road,
Notting Hill,
London W11 1QU

Alcoholics Anonymous
PO Box 1, Stonebow House,
Stonebow,
York YO1 2NJ
Tel; 01904 644026/7/8/9

Positively Women (HIV/AIDS)
5 Sebastian Street,
London EC1V 0HE
Tel; 0171 490 5515

Terence Higgins Trust (HIV/AIDS)
52–54 Grays Inn Road,
London EC1
Tel; 0171 242 1010

Relate (Marriage Guidance and relationship counselling)
Herbert Gray College,
Little Church Street,
Rugby CV21 3AP
Tel; 01788 573241